POSTWAR AMERICA
THE POSTWAR BOOM
by Brienna Rossiter

FOCUS READERS
NAVIGATOR

WWW.FOCUSREADERS.COM

Copyright © 2024 by Focus Readers®, Mendota Heights, MN 55120. All rights reserved. No part of this book may be reproduced or utilized in any form or by any means without written permission from the publisher.

Focus Readers is distributed by North Star Editions:
sales@northstareditions.com | 888-417-0195

Produced for Focus Readers by Red Line Editorial.

Content Consultant: Leonard Steinhorn, Professor of Communication and Affiliate Professor of History, American University

Photographs ©: AP Images, cover, 1, 12; Russell Lee/National Archives, 4–5; Marion S. Trikosko/Library of Congress, 7; Wikimedia Commons, 8; Robert Clover/AP Images, 10–11; Thomas J. O'Halloran/Library of Congress, 15; Hulton Archive/Archive Photos/Getty Images, 16–17; Angelo Rizzuto/Library of Congress, 18; Robert Kradin/AP Images, 21; Bettmann/Getty Images, 23, 28; John Lent/AP Images, 24–25; Matty Zimmerman/AP Images, 27

Library of Congress Cataloging-in-Publication Data
Names: Rossiter, Brienna, author.
Title: The postwar boom / by Brienna Rossiter.
Description: Mendota Heights, MN : Focus Readers, 2024. | Series: Postwar America | Includes bibliographical references and index. | Audience: Grades 4-6
Identifiers: LCCN 2023033090 (print) | LCCN 2023033091 (ebook) | ISBN 9798889980438 (hardcover) | ISBN 9798889980865 (paperback) | ISBN 9798889981671 (pdf) | ISBN 9798889981299 (ebook)
Subjects: LCSH: United States--Economic conditions--1945---Juvenile literature. | United States--Economic policy--1945-1960--Juvenile literature.
Classification: LCC HC106.5 .R67 2024 (print) | LCC HC106.5 (ebook) | DDC 330.973--dc23/eng/20230801
LC record available at https://lccn.loc.gov/2023033090
LC ebook record available at https://lccn.loc.gov/2023033091

Printed in the United States of America
Mankato, MN
012024

ABOUT THE AUTHOR
Brienna Rossiter is a writer and editor who lives in Minnesota. She loves learning about history.

TABLE OF CONTENTS

CHAPTER 1
Many Changes 5

CHAPTER 2
Jobs and Opportunities 11

CHAPTER 3
Housing 17

VOICES FROM THE PAST
Levittowns 22

CHAPTER 4
Legacy 25

Focus on the Postwar Boom • 30
Glossary • 31
To Learn More • 32
Index • 32

CHAPTER 1

MANY CHANGES

During World War II (1939–1945), the US **economy** grew rapidly. Factories churned out weapons for soldiers. When the war ended, demand for weapons dropped. So, factories made products for ordinary people. Many experts were worried. In the past, returning soldiers had struggled to find work. After World

Some companies produced refrigerators after making weapons during the war.

War I (1914–1918), many **veterans** couldn't pay for basic needs. Experts feared a similar problem could happen again. If it did, factories might have to close. Many people could lose their jobs.

Instead, the opposite happened. The US economy continued to boom. Factories produced millions of cars. They also made toys, appliances, and other household items. People were eager to buy all these products.

Before the war, the **Great Depression** had kept many people from being able to afford things. Then the war brought other limits. Some items were **rationed**. Others weren't produced at all. After the

By 1959, more than 85 percent of US homes had a TV set.

war, those limits ended. People rushed to buy things they hadn't been able to get before.

Advertising helped, too. Companies tried to convince people to buy things based on wants rather than needs. Sales of TVs and other appliances skyrocketed.

Many people made big purchases, too. They bought homes and cars. Some people had saved money during the war. Others got government assistance. New laws and programs helped. One was

BABY BOOM

The red portion shows a higher birth rate after the war.

the G.I. Bill. It gave veterans money for homes, education, and more.

All these changes increased many people's standard of living. Between 1945 and 1965, the average family's income doubled. More people became part of the middle class. Many young adults got married and started families. Between 1946 and 1958, more than 70 million babies were born in the United States.

However, not everyone could access these new opportunities. More than 23 percent of Americans still lived in poverty. And programs like the G.I. Bill mainly helped white families. People of color were less likely to receive benefits.

CHAPTER 2

JOBS AND OPPORTUNITIES

The G.I. Bill helped returning soldiers in several ways. For example, it helped them get health care. It helped them get home loans, too. It also provided unemployment benefits. Veterans could receive up to a year of training and payments while they were looking for jobs.

President Franklin D. Roosevelt signed the G.I. Bill in June 1944.

 In 1947, nearly half of all college students were veterans.

The G.I. Bill also helped veterans pay for education. By 1951, more than two million veterans had gone to college. Millions of others had received job training. This education helped them get higher-paying jobs. They could better support themselves and their families.

The G.I. Bill was supposed to be for all veterans. However, women and people of color were much less likely to receive benefits. They often faced discrimination. When they applied for benefits, local officials often denied them. Some women and people of color did get funding. But their options for schools and programs were limited.

Some schools accepted male students first. Few spots were left for female students. Other schools didn't accept women at all. **Segregation** barred Black students from many colleges. Other schools didn't let Black students use the same equipment as white students. That kept Black students from entering certain jobs or programs. For example, a school in Illinois accepted Black students. But they couldn't study plumbing, electricity, or printing.

These differences played a role in the jobs people got. Women and people of color were often told to study less-skilled

UNEQUAL ACCESS

The G.I. Bill became law in 1944. Under the law, states gave out benefits. Southern lawmakers had pushed for this rule. At the time, the South had many Jim Crow laws. These laws supported segregation. By putting states in charge, lawmakers gave power to local officials. That way, officials could deny benefits to Black people. Many officials did.

Many white people supported segregation. They protested attempts to change it.

work. So, they tended to get lower-paying jobs. Meanwhile, white men were more likely to work in higher-paying fields. Those pay differences affected people's opportunities.

15

CHAPTER 3

HOUSING

Other postwar changes involved housing. In 1945, only 40 percent of Americans owned homes. By 1960, 60 percent did. Many buyers got help from the G.I. Bill. Others received loans from the US government.

Companies began building many homes quickly. New suburbs popped up

In the 1950s, the number of people living in suburbs rose by 47 percent.

 By 1960, three-fourths of all US families owned cars.

around cities. During the 1950s, more than 18 million Americans moved into these areas. This shift was linked to many other changes. For example, as people bought homes in the suburbs, they also bought cars. The automobile industry boomed. So did sales of appliances.

However, most families that moved to the suburbs were white. Banks often denied loans to Black families. Some lenders also used a process called redlining. This practice began in the 1930s. Lenders used color-coded maps. They decided which people would receive

CAR CRAZE

Many suburban homes were far from where people worked. So, people needed cars to travel back and forth. In the 1950s, governments created many new roads and highways for them to drive on. Meanwhile, people in cities tended to use public transportation. Those systems often lacked funding. Also, some neighborhoods were torn down to build new roads. These places were often where immigrants and people of color lived.

loans based on where they lived. Some areas were colored red and called "risky." Those neighborhoods had mainly Black residents. Banks wouldn't give loans to people who lived there.

Racial covenants played a role, too. These phrases were written into documents that let people buy or rent homes. They often said that only white people could live there. So, many areas became more segregated. People of color were more likely to stay in cities. Meanwhile, many businesses also moved to the suburbs.

These differences had many impacts. It was much harder for people of color

Cities often lost money as people and businesses moved out.

to buy homes. In New York and northern New Jersey, the G.I. Bill supported 67,000 home loans. Fewer than 100 of these loans went to people of color. Where families live affects job opportunities and where children go to school. Schools in areas with less funding often struggle to offer good educations.

21

VOICES FROM THE PAST

LEVITTOWNS

After the war, Levitt and Sons became famous. The company created mass-produced houses. To save time and money, they built rows of identical houses. These neighborhoods were known as Levittowns.

The first Levittown was built between 1946 and 1951. The New York neighborhood had more than 17,000 houses. Eugene Burnett applied for one. But he was turned down because he was Black.

Like many suburbs, Levittowns had rules about who could buy houses. Homes couldn't "be used or occupied by any person other than members of the Caucasian race."[1] In 1948, the US Supreme Court ruled against limits like this. But Levittowns still avoided selling and renting homes to non-white families. When people of color did move in, some white families left. Others

At one point, Levitt and Sons was making 36 houses per day.

formed mobs. Over time, people worked to change the racist rules. But Levittowns remained mainly white for years.

Meanwhile, Black families like Burnett's lived in other neighborhoods. "We didn't have many other choices," he said. To him, Levittowns were "symbolic of segregation in America."[2]

1. Bruce Lambert. "At 50, Levittown contends with its legacy of bias." *New York Times*. New York Times, 28 Dec. 1997. Web. 10 Apr. 2023.
2. Ibid.

CHAPTER 4

LEGACY

Many people saw the postwar years as a time of peace and wealth. They believed businesses helped improve people's lives. Wealth did increase. Between 1940 and 1950, the **gross national product** rose by $100 billion. The United States became the richest country in the world. There were changes

Union membership was higher in the 1950s than in any other decade in US history.

to labor, too. **Unions** helped workers get better pay. However, not all people had access to these gains.

People also faced pressure not to disagree or stand out. If they did, they could be punished or silenced. Fear of **Communism** was one reason. At the time, many US leaders saw Communism as a threat. They feared that Communist countries would attack the United States. People accused of being Communists could lose their jobs.

The media set limits, too. Newspapers and magazines were afraid to print risky ideas. TV and radio stations were also careful about the views they aired.

Edward R. Murrow was a famous broadcaster. He cared about getting good information to the public.

Even so, some people spoke out. The civil rights movement was an important example. It fought discrimination in voting, housing, education, employment, and other areas. Several key events took place during the 1950s. One was *Brown v. Board of Education*. This Supreme

US soldiers guarded the Little Rock Nine as they went to and from school.

Court decision made segregation illegal in public schools. Students such as the Little Rock Nine attended formerly white schools. The Montgomery bus boycott was also important. It helped end segregation on public transportation.

Other people opposed different kinds of social pressure. Many writers, poets, and musicians urged people to think for themselves. In addition, some writers described the problems women faced. These views set the stage for later movements. Those movements continue to impact the United States today.

ROLES FOR WOMEN

Postwar media often promoted strict gender roles. Women were expected to stay home and raise families. Some people spoke out against this idea. Betty Friedan's book *The Feminine Mystique* was one example. She interviewed many women. Most had homes, families, and money. But they felt stuck or lonely. Friedan said unrealistic gender roles were to blame. The women needed more opportunities.

FOCUS ON
THE POSTWAR BOOM

Write your answers on a separate piece of paper.

1. Write a paragraph summarizing the main ideas of Chapter 1.

2. Which postwar change do you think had the biggest impact? Why?

3. When did the G.I. Bill become law?
    - **A.** 1944
    - **B.** 1957
    - **C.** 1965

4. If public transportation receives low funding, what effect would that most likely have?
    - **A.** Governments would receive more money to spend on roads.
    - **B.** Cities would struggle to pay for repairs to trains and buses.
    - **C.** More people would want to ride public transportation.

Answer key on page 32.

GLOSSARY

Communism
A political idea that calls for all property to be owned by the public.

economy
The system of goods, services, money, and jobs in a certain place.

Great Depression
A time from 1929 to 1939 when banks failed, economies struggled, and many people lacked money and jobs.

gross national product
The total amount of goods and services a country produces.

rationed
Limited the amount of something that people can buy.

segregation
The separation of groups of people based on race or other factors.

unions
Organizations that protect the rights of workers.

veterans
People who have served in the military.

TO LEARN MORE

BOOKS

Doudna, Kelly. *Automobiles: From Henry Ford to Elon Musk*. Minneapolis: Abdo Publishing, 2019.

Green, Amanda Jackson. *Hidden Black History: From Juneteenth to Redlining*. Minneapolis: Lerner Publications, 2021.

Harris, Duchess, with Kate Conley. *The Great Migration*. Minneapolis: Abdo Publishing, 2020.

NOTE TO EDUCATORS

Visit **www.focusreaders.com** to find lesson plans, activities, links, and other resources related to this title.

INDEX

Baby Boom, 8
Brown v. Board of Education, 27–28

cars, 6, 8, 18–19
civil rights movement, 27
Communism, 26

economy, 5–6
education, 9, 12, 21, 27

factories, 5–6

gender roles, 29
G.I. Bill, 9, 11–14, 17, 21
Great Depression, 6

Jim Crow, 14

Levittowns, 22–23
loans, 11, 17, 19–21

media, 26, 29
Montgomery bus boycott, 28

people of color, 9, 13–14, 19–21, 22

racial covenants, 20
redlining, 19–20

segregation, 13–14, 20, 23, 28
suburbs, 17–20, 22

Answer Key: 1. Answers will vary; 2. Answers will vary; 3. A; 4. B